THE TANIWHA OF WELLINGTON HARBOUR

MOIRA WAIRAMA

ILLUSTRATED BY
BRUCE POTTER

PUFFIN BOOKS

In ancient times
in Aotearoa,
there was a
beautiful
lake in which there
dwelt two
monstrous
taniwha.

Their names
were **Whātaitai**
and **Ngake**.

Whātaitai was an easygoing taniwha. He liked to **cruise** slowly around the lake, stopping often to eat the **fat,** juicy eels at Te Awa-kairangi river mouth. After his meal he would **stretch** himself out to sleep in the sun on Pito-one beach.

Ngake, however, spent most of his time **speeding** around the lake as fast as he could swim. His favourite game was leaping over Matiu Island and doing spectacular *belly flops.*

One day Ngake said to his friend, 'E hoa, I'm bored.

I want to leave this lake and journey out into the great ocean. Will you come with me?' Whātaitai laughed.

'You must be pōrangi.

There's no way to swim out of this lake. It's surrounded by land.' And he laughed even harder.

Ngake became angry. 'I'm not pōrangi!' he snarled.

'I'm big and strong and I will break through the land to the sea.

'Come with me!'

Whātaitai stopped laughing.
'What if you kill
        yourself, Ngake?'
he hissed in fear.

'I would be alone.'
'Once I have gone you will be
        alone anyway,' replied Ngake.

'E hoa. Come with me!'

'NO!' howled Whātaitai.
'This is our home.'

The two taniwha began to
argue loudly, their tails slashing
back and forth, creating
gigantic waves that crashed
upon the shores of the lake.

Finally, with a cry of
frustration, Whātaitai
turned his back on his
friend and swam away.

Snarling with annoyance,
Ngake flicked his long tail
and began to swim in great circles
around
the lake.

Faster and faster
he went until he had
reached full speed.
Suddenly he turned
sharply and sped
southwards.

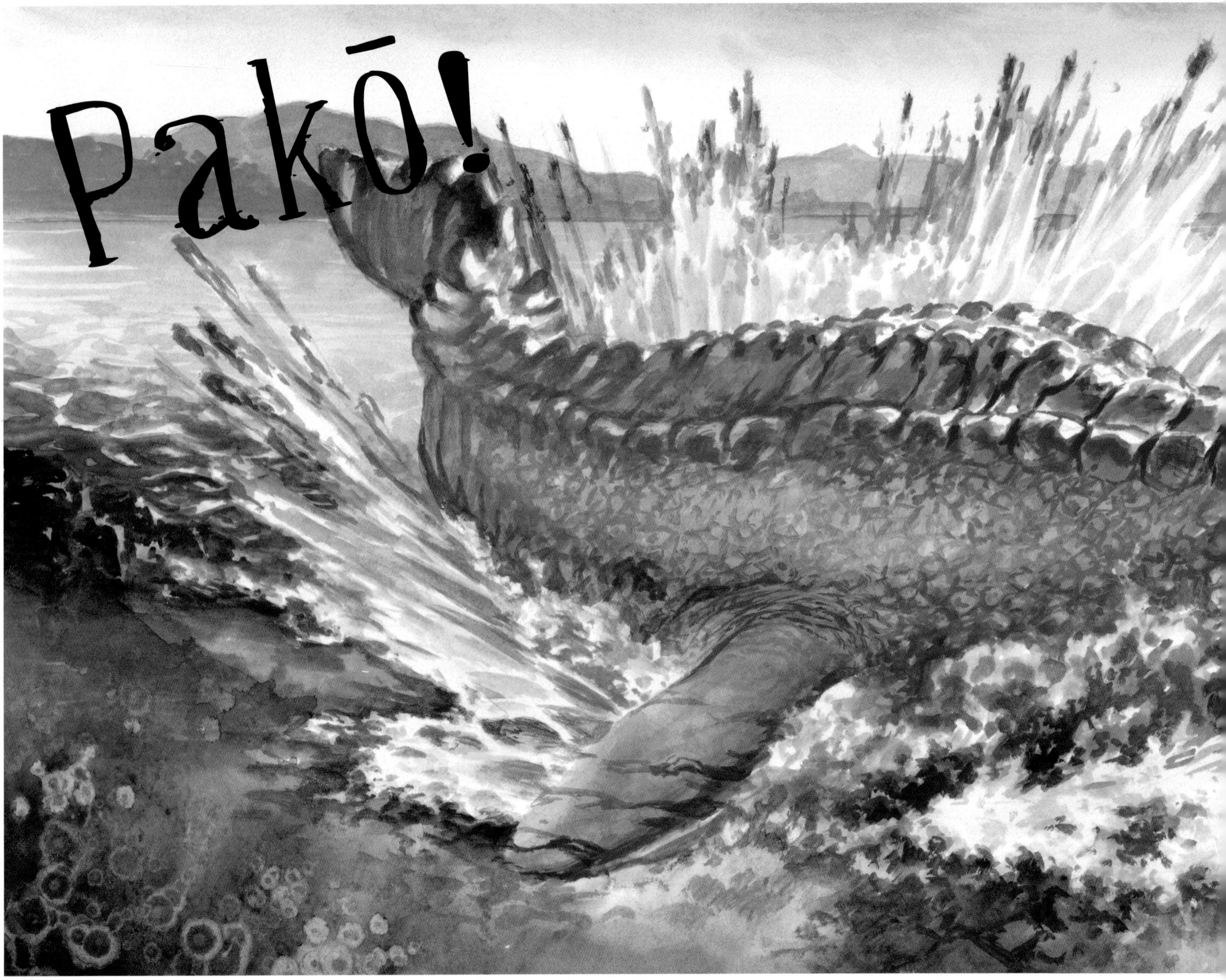
Pakō!

N gake's powerful body
crashed
into the land,
shattering earth and rocks
in all directions.
Pieces of his flesh were ripped
from his side and his blood **flowed**
into the water,
turning it dark red.

As the land crumbled about him,
Ngake forced his way through to
the vast ocean. Although the salt water
stung his wounds, it also stopped the bleeding.

With a triumphant
roar

he surged up out of the
water and, turning his head,
he looked back towards Whātaitai.

Then with a

joyous flick of his tail, he turned and was gone.

As Ngake's roar echoed around the hills,
the sea surged through the
jagged gap
he had created,
changing the lake into a harbour.
Whātaitai watched in shocked surprise
as Tohorā the whale,
Aihe the dolphin, Mangō the shark
and many other sea creatures
entered his home.
He realised that Ngake's leaving
had changed everything.

'I should have gone with him,' moaned Whātaitai.

'Maybe it's not too late?'

Gingerly, he swam towards where
Ngake had broken free.
The water was still red with blood.

'Auē, I can't swim through that' he wailed in horror.

As the days passed, Whātaitai's
sorrow deepened. He tried to cheer himself up by
swallowing an enormous meal of slippery eels,
but it didn't help.

He tried to sleep in the sun on Pito-one beach,
but since he was facing the gap where his friend
had broken free, that only made him sadder.
As he lay there, an astonishing
idea crept into his mind.

'I'm as strong as Ngake.
I could make my own
way out to the ocean.'

Rolling himself into the water,

Whātaitai began to
swim towards the
small bay to the west of
where Ngake had left.

'I'd better swim **faster'**

he puffed as he approached the land,
but at that very moment he felt his
puku scraping on the bottom of the harbour.

Whātaitai did not
understand that a harbour has tides,
and since the tide was out,
he suddenly found himself **stuck.**
He tried to wriggle backwards
but the more he **wriggled,**
the more he sank into the sandy floor of the harbour.

'I must **break** free' he thought desperately,

arching his back and throwing back his head.
But it was no good.
'I'm stuck,' wailed Whātaitai.
'Help me!'
But there was no one
to hear his call.

For many lonely centuries
       Whātaitai lay
           beneath the waves,
           imprisoned in his sandy seabed,
feeding on any fish that swam
                close enough for him to snap up.

When the famous Māori explorer,
           Kupe, discovered the harbour,
Whātaitai tried to call to him,
but Kupe heard nothing as he and his people
           sailed away across the loud, slapping

waves.

More lonely years passed and
Whātaitai dreamed of Ngake returning.
One day his heart
stirred with hope
as a long shadow crossed
the sea above him. But it was not Ngake.

It was a fleet of waka carrying the
Ngāi Tara people into the harbour.

'Please stay'
Whātaitai called from
beneath the waves.

Although the Ngāi Tara could not hear him,
they did settle in the harbour, which they named
Te Whanga-nui-ā-Tara,
after their great ancestor.
It was only when they were building
their hilltop pā that they noticed the
taniwha trapped in the
bay below them.

'Help me!'
Whātaitai called,
but the people knew there
was no way they could
free a taniwha.
Instead they comforted
him with the haunting
melody of their flutes and
their passionate waiata.

Then one still and cloudless day,
Whātaitai suddenly felt the sand
around him shudder and shift.

'What is happening?'
he cried anxiously, as the
sea swirled wildly
and the harbour floor beneath
him was thrust
upwards
by a giant
earthquake.

Lifted above the sea,
Whātaitai struggled without success
to roll himself back into the water.
His breath became laboured as
exhaustion overcame him.

'Ngake'
he gasped and then lay still.

From his body a beautiful
white bird flew up and
alighted on the hilltop across from
the Ngāi Tara pā.

'Auuuuuuuuuueeeeeeeeee

cried the spirit
of Whātaitai.

His cry brought the Ngāi Tara
people rushing from their pā just in
time to see the spirit bird disappearing
north towards the ancient
homeland of Hawaiki.

As soon as it departed,
a great wave carrying
sand, rocks and driftwood crashed
down upon the taniwha's
body, burying it forever.

The Ngāi Tara people named that
place Whātaitai in his memory.